UNITED STATES
NAVAL ACADEMY
Where Severn Joins the Tide

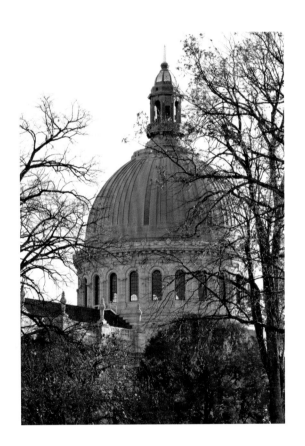

UNITED STATES NAVAL ACADEMY
ALUMNI ASSOCIATION

UNITED STATES NAVAL ACADEMY
FOUNDATION

Produced for the

Published by

203 W. Belmont Drive
Allen, Texas 75013
972-747-7866
FAX 972-747-0226
www.dsapubs.com

Publisher: Duff Tussing

Associate Publisher: Steve Boston

Photography: Alison Harbaugh

Design: Donnie Jones, The Press Group

Printed in Canada

PUBLISHER'S DATA

United State Naval Academy — Where Severn Joins the Tide

Library of Congress Control Number: 2008910298

ISBN Number: 978-0-9818229-8-3

First Printing 2008

10 9 8 7 6 5 4 3 2 1

United States Naval Academy

Where Severn Joins the Tide

photography by Alison Harbaugh
foreword by ADM Carlisle A. Trost '53, USN (Ret.)

Like many Naval Academy graduates, I chose to retire in Annapolis because of the Naval Academy. The Yard means many things to me, as I am sure it does to my classmates, those who went before us, and those who will follow us. The Academy's environment shaped our first steps towards becoming a commissioned officer, and it was here that our core values were developed so that we could be better prepared to serve our nation. Since its founding in 1845, the Naval Academy has provided the United States with thousands of leaders of great distinction who served not only in the military but also in all walks of life.

Living in Annapolis has afforded me the opportunity, and indeed the privilege, to walk the same bricks that I walked upon in the early 1950s as a midshipman from Illinois. I marvel at the timelessness of Ernest Flagg's late 19th-century design. The buildings have been upgraded over time with fiber optics and other technology to further assist in our mission to develop today's midshipmen mentally, morally and physically. The government has provided for the Academy's basic needs, but private dollars have provided the margin of excellence that makes the Academy the great institution it is today.

And so this book captures the Naval Academy that was designed by Mr. Flagg, while also capturing the generosity of its many benefactors –Alumni, parents and friends – who have given to support today's Brigade of Midshipmen with new facilities and programs.

No matter where you are now, join me on a tour of today's Naval Academy that is better prepared to serve future generations because of your support.

ADM C.A.H. Trost, USN (Ret.) '53
Chairman of the Board
U.S. Naval Academy Alumni Association

CONTENTS

UNITED STATES NAVAL ACADEMY
fall

U.S. Naval Academy Chapel

Porter Road Quarters

Stribling Walk

Tecumseh

The Brigade of Midshipmen

Bill XXXII, Bill XXXIII

Zimmerman Bandstand

Mahan Hall & Sampson Hall

Herndon Monument

Bancroft Hall

Mahan Hall

Buchanan House

Herndon Monument

September 12
1857.

Mahan Hall

United States
Naval Academy
winter

Porter Road Quarters

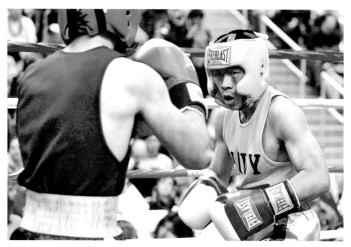

Japanese Pagoda in front of Luce Hall

Bancroft Hall

U.S. Naval Academy Chapel

Above and Right *Chapel Interior*

The Unah P. Levy Center and Jewish Chapel

The Mexican Monument

Sampson Hall

Buchanan House

United States Naval Academy
spring

Navy- Marine Corps Memorial Stadium

Halligan Hall

Wesley Brown Field House

Ring Dance

Alumni Hall

Ward Hall

Above and Left *Herndon Monument*

Halsey Field House

Thornton D. and Elizabeth S. Hooper Brigade Sports Complex

Alumni Hall

Robert Crown Sailing Center

Color Parade

Hat Toss

Bill the Goat

Hubbard Hall

RANGER ★ ★ SERAPIS ★ ALLIANCE

JOHN PAUL JONES
1747   1792
UNITED STATES NA
1775   1783
E OUR NAVY ITS EARLIEST
OF HEROISM AND VICT
RECTED BY THE CONGRESS

The Crypt of John Paul Jones

UNITED STATES
NAVAL ACADEMY
summer

The Enterprise Bell

The Glenn Warner Soccer Facility

THIS LIGHT IS DEDICATED
TO THE SAFE RETURN
OF ALL THOSE WHO GO
DOWN TO THE SEA IN SHIPS
THE CLASS OF 1948

Admiral Ben Moreell

Triton Light

Armel-Leftwich Visitor Center

Bancroft Hall

Admiral James B. Stockdale

Dahlgren Hall

Bancroft Hall

Bancroft Hall

Vice Admiral William P. Lawrence

Facing Page *Memorial Hall*

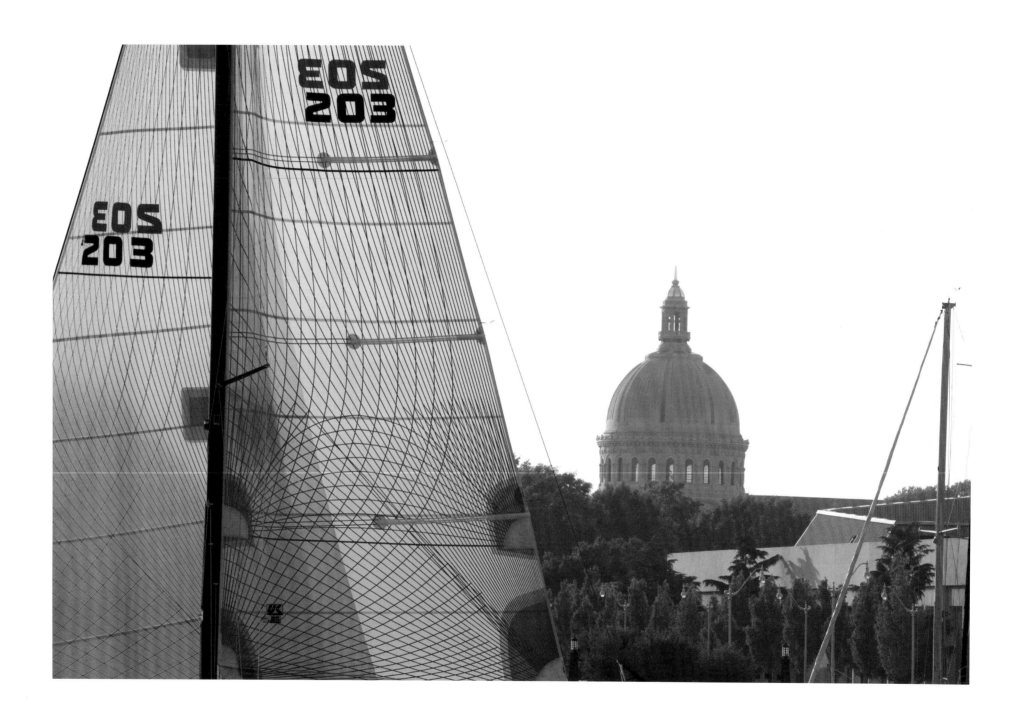

Officers' & Faculty Club

Porter Road Quarters

Above and Below *Yard Patrol Craft*

UNITED STATES NAVAL ACADEMY

annapolis

The State House

The Maryland Inn

City Dock Area

O'Brien's Main Street

U.S. Post Office

Thurgood Marshall Memorial Statue — Lawyers Mall

UNITED STATES
NAVAL ACADEMY
alumni house

Class of 1952 Ballroom

Ogle Hall

1907 Room

1923 Room

1921 Area

The 1967 Patio

UNITED STATES NAVAL ACADEMY
ALUMNI ASSOCIATION

UNITED STATES NAVAL ACADEMY
FOUNDATION

Founded in 1886

The course set by Alumni Association founders in 1886 rings true today as the Alumni Association serves and supports the United States, the naval service, the Naval Academy and its alumni: by furthering the highest standards at the Naval Academy; by seeking out, informing, encouraging and assisting outstanding, qualified young men and women to pursue careers as officers through the Naval Academy; and by initiating and sponsoring activities which perpetuate the history, traditions, memories and growth of the Naval Academy and bind alumni together in support of the highest ideals of command, citizenship and government.

With a primary focus on friend raising, the Alumni Association promotes informed advocacy for today's Naval Academy and Brigade of Midshipmen among its many constituents—alumni, parents and friends. The Association keeps its more than 52,000 members informed through a network of 100 chapters around the world, 75 active class organizations, and 84 parent clubs. The Association web site, *www.usna.com*; *Shipmate* magazine; and other electronic and print publication are the primary communications tools, while value-added benefits and services build affinity to the Naval Academy.

The original Naval Academy Foundation, formed in 1944, set out to support athletic programs at the Naval Academy through scholarships, grants and awards. In 1999, the Foundation and the Naval Academy Endowment Trust merged to form the sole fundraising entity for the Naval Academy, now known as the United States Naval Academy Foundation.

The complementary mission of the Naval Academy Foundation is to support, promote and advance the mission of the Naval Academy by working in conjunction with Academy leadership to identify strategic and institutional priorities and by raising, managing and disbursing private gift funds that provide a margin of excellence in support of the nation's premier leadership institution. The Athletic and Scholarship Programs division is a significant element of the Foundation. This division promotes athletic excellence at the Naval Academy through a comprehensive preparatory school scholarship program and through privately funded grants to athletic and physical development programs for which government funds are not appropriate or not available.

In today's highly competitive world, funding through private gifts is essential to the strategic advancement of a dynamic learning environment that encourages midshipmen to anticipate, prepare for and ultimately lead and serve. The transformational aspects of private giving is seen throughout the Yard in new or renovated buildings, privately-funded faculty positions, or programs which enhance the education of the Brigade of Midshipmen. The Foundation continues to build upon the momentum and achievements in a post-campaign period and work to sustain a culture of philanthropy.

With more than 120 years of history and progress, the U.S. Naval Academy Alumni Association & Foundation are proud to celebrate traditions while partnering with the Naval Academy to sustain a margin of excellence needed to secure a bright future.

U.S. Naval Academy Alumni Association
247 King George Street • Annapolis, MD 21402
410-295-4000 • www.usna.com